MW00719512

To:

From:

Copyright © 2001 by Kathy Wagoner
Cover and internal design © 2001 by Sourcebooks, Inc.

Published by Sourcebooks, Inc.
P.O. Box 4410, Naperville, Illinois 60567-4410
(630) 961-3900
FAX: (630) 961-2168
www.sourcebooks.com

ISBN 1-57071-701-X

Printed and bound in the United States of America
VP   10 9 8 7 6 5 4

365

KISSES

by Kathy Wagoner

SOURCEBOOKS CASABLANCA™
AN IMPRINT OF SOURCEBOOKS, INC.®
NAPERVILLE, ILLINOIS

LOVE looks not with the eyes, but with the heart.

—William Shakespeare

1

2

The best portion
of a good man is
his little, nameless,
unremembered acts
of kindness and **LOVE**.

—William Wordsworth

3

LOVE knows no winter; no, no! It is and remains the sign of spring.

—Ludwig Tieck

LOVE grows by giving.
The **LOVE** we give away is
the only **LOVE** we keep.
The only way to retain
LOVE is to give it away.

—Elbert Hubbard

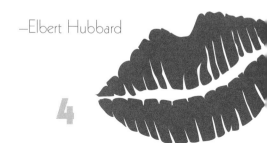

4

5

Respect is **LOVE**

in plain clothes.

—Frankie Byrne

LOVE is the emotion that catches you unaware and causes you to laugh when you're discouraged and cry when you want to be tough.

Bitterness imprisons life;

LOVE releases it.

—Harry Emerson Fosdick

7

8

We don't **LOVE** qualities, we **LOVE** persons; sometimes by reasons of their defects as well as of their qualities.

–Jacques Maritain

9

The supreme happiness
in life is the conviction
that we are **LOVED**.

–Victor Hugo

A **LOVE** song is just a

caress set to music.

—Sigmund Romburg

10

11

It is **LOVE,** not reason, that is stronger than death.

—Thomas Merton

LOVE is no simple feeling;

it is truth, even the

greatest truth of our lives.

12

While faith makes all things possible, it is **LOVE** that makes all things easy.

—Evan H. Hopkins

13

14

A friendship that like
love is warm; A **LOVE**
like friendship, steady.

—Thomas Moore

15

There is no **LOVE**
which does not
become help.

—Paul Tillich

LOVE can hope where

reason will despair.

—George, Baron Lyttle

16

17

As selfishness and complaint
crowd the mind, so **LOVE**
with its joy clears and
sharpens the vision.

—Helen Keller

Familiar acts are beautiful

through **LOVE.**

—Percy Bysshe Shelley

18

LOVE is born of faith,

lives on hope, and

dies of charity.

—Gian Carlo Menotti

19

One makes mistakes:
that is life. But it is never
quite a mistake to
have **LOVED.**

—Romain Roland

Whoso **LOVES**

believes the impossible.

—Elizabeth Barrett Browning

LOVE is a powerful
noun but an even
stronger verb.

22

23

LOVE dies only
when growth stops.

—Pearl S. Buck

LOVE is like quicksilver in the hand. Leave the fingers open and it stays in the palm; clutch it, and it darts away.

—Dorothy Parker

24

LOVE is a gross
exaggeration of the
difference between one
person and everybody else.

—George Bernard Shaw

25

When silence speaks
for **LOVE** she has
much to say.

—Richard Garnett

27

Marriage is that
relation between man and
woman in which the
independence is equal, the
dependence mutual, and
the obligation reciprocal.

—Louis Kaufman Anspacher

LOVE consists in this,

that two solitudes

protect and touch

and greet each other.

–Rainer Maria Rilke

28

29

LOVE is all we have,
the only way that each
can help the other.

—Euripides

Could we but think
with the intensity we
LOVE with, we might
do great things.

–P. J. Bailey

30

The best and most
beautiful things in the
world cannot be seen or
even touched. They must
be felt with the heart.

—Helen Keller

Yes, **LOVE** indeed
is light from heaven;
A spark of that immortal
fire which angels shared.

—George, Lord Byron

To **LOVE** and be **LOVED** is to feel the sun from both sides.

—David Viscott

LOVE is what
you've been through
with somebody.

—James Thurber

34

35

It is the nature of **LOVE**

to work in a thousand

different ways.

—Saint Teresa

Friendship is a strong and habitual inclination in two persons to promote the good and happiness of one another.

—Eustace Budgell

36

It is sad not to be **LOVED,**

but it is much sadder not

to be able to **LOVE.**

—Miguel de Unamuno

37

To **LOVE** abundantly

is to live abundantly,

and to **LOVE** forever

is to live forever.

—Henry Drummond

39

LOVE is **LOVE'S**

own reward.

–John Dryden

Yesterday's hurt

is today's understanding

woven into tomorrow's

LOVE.

40

41

A **LOVING** heart is the beginning of all knowledge.

—Thomas Carlyle

LOVE is not a mere emotion or sentiment. It is the lucid and ardent responses of the whole person to a value that is revealed to him as perfect.

—Thomas Merton

42

To be **LOVED,**
be **LOVABLE.**

–Ovid

43

44

Because they have been in **LOVE** they have survived everything that life could throw at them, even their own failures.

—Peter Ustinov

45

Adam could not be
happy even in Paradise
without Eve.

–Lord John Lubbock Avery

LOVE is more

just than justice.

—Henry Ward Beecher

46

47

There is only one happiness
in life, to **LOVE** and
be **LOVED.**

–George Sand

A pennyweight o' **LOVE**

is worth a pound o' law.

—Scottish proverb

48

Can there be a **LOVE**
which does not make
demands on its object?

—Confucius

49

50

It has been said that
we cannot really **LOVE**
anybody at whom
we never laugh.

—Afnes Repplier

51

There is no heaven
like mutual **LOVE.**

—George Granville

It takes two flints

to make a fire.

–Louisa May Alcott

52

53

LOVE must be learned
and learned again;
there is no end to it.

—Katherine Anne Portor

The understanding smile
of an old wife to her husband
is one of the **LOVELIEST**
things in the world.

—Booth Tarkington

The course of
true **LOVE** never
did run smooth.

—William Shakespeare

56

There is nothing
ridiculous in **LOVE.**

—Ella Wheeler Wilcox

57

If you **LOVE** a person,
you **LOVE** him in his
stark reality, and refuse
to shut your eyes to
his defects and errors.

—John MacMurray

When the evening of
this life comes, we shall
be judged on **LOVE.**

—St. John of the Cross

58

59

When one is in **LOVE,**

a cliff becomes a meadow.

—Ethiopian proverb

LOVE can be seen
clearly from a distance.

Never look for

a worm in the

apple of your eye.

—Langston Hughes

61

There is no surprise
more magical than the
surprise of being
LOVED.

–Charles Morgan

63

LOVE starts when
another person's needs
become more important
than your own.

It's not **LOVE'S**
going hurts my days,
But that it went
in little ways.

—Edna St. Vincent Millay

64

65

LOVE should be a tree
whose roots are deep in the
earth, but whose branches
extend into heaven.

—Bertrand Russell

LOVE is the triumph

of the imagination

over intelligence.

–H. L. Mencken

The **LOVE** we give
and the **LOVE** we
receive give shape and
texture to our lives.

67

There is a wealth
of unexpressed **LOVE**
in the world.

—Arthur Hopkins

69

When you're in **LOVE**
you feel that you have
found the other half
of yourself, the half you
have needed in order
to become complete.

One pardons to the degree that one **LOVES.**

—François de La Rouchefoucauld

70

71

The first duty of **LOVE**

is to listen.

LOVE is not a matter of counting the years—it's making the years count.

—Jack Smith

72

There is no soul that does
not respond to **LOVE,**
for the soul of man is a
guest that has gone hungry
these centuries back.

—Maurice Maeterlinck

74

It is difficult to know at what moment **LOVE** begins; it is less difficult to know it has begun.

–H. W. Longfellow

One must not lose desires.

They are mighty stimulants

to creativeness, to **LOVE,**

and to long life.

—Alexander A. Bogomoletz

If Jack's in **LOVE,**
he's no judge of
Jill's beauty.

—Benjamin Franklin

76

77

Is there a spirit wounded

so deeply that **LOVE**

cannot heal it?

LOVE is the symbol
of eternity.

—Madame de Staël

78

Were it not for **LOVE,**
Poor life would be a ship
not worth launching.

—Edwin Arlington Robinson

80

So long as we **LOVE,** we serve. So long as we are **LOVED** by others, we are indispensable; and no man is useless while he has a friend.

—Robert Louis Stevenson

Wherever you are it is your own friends who make your world.

—William James

You don't **LOVE** a
man for what he says,
but **LOVE** what he says
because you **LOVE** him.

—Andre Maurois

82

83

The moments when you have
really lived are the moments
when you have done things in
the spirit of **LOVE.**

—Henry Drummond

Happiness and Beauty
are **LOVE'S** children.

—Rita Hayden

84

Grumbling is the

death of **LOVE.**

—Marlene Dietrich

85

86

Above our life

we **LOVE** a

steadfast friend.

—Christopher Marlowe

87

When you **LOVE** someone all your saved up wishes come out.

—Elizabeth Bowen

LOVE is a

motivational energy.

89

LOVE does not cause suffering;

what causes it is the sense of

our ownership, which is

LOVE'S opposite.

—Antoine de Saint-Exupery

A very small degree
of hope is sufficient to
cause the birth of **LOVE.**

—Stendahl

90

Never the time and
the place and the **LOVED**
one all together!

—Robert Browning

91

I never knew how to worship until I knew how to **LOVE.**

—Henry Ward Beecher

All, everything
that I understand,
I understand only
because I **LOVE.**

–Leo Tolstoy

LOVE is a canvas

furnished by Nature

and embroidered

by imagination.

—Voltaire

94

95

LOVE conquers all things;

let us too surrender

to **LOVE.**

—Virgil

Take away **LOVE** and

our earth is a tomb.

—Robert Browning

96

There is only one sort of **LOVE,** but there are a thousand copies.

—François de La Rouchefoucauld

97

98

Try to reason about
LOVE and you will
lose your reason.

—French proverb

Whoever **LOVES**
true life, will **LOVE**
true **LOVE.**

—Elizabeth Barrett Browning

I know of no better definition of **LOVE** than the one given by Proust—"**LOVE** is space and time measured by the heart."

—Gian Carlo Menotti

100

101

We are all born for **LOVE;**

it is the principal of our

existence and its only end.

—Benjamin Disraeli

Friendship is **LOVE**

with understanding.

102

Let those **LOVE** now who
never **LOVED** before;
Let those who always **LOVED,**
now **LOVE** the more.

—Thomas Parnell

103

Your **LOVE** shines in

my heart as sun that

shines upon the earth.

—Eleanor Di Guilio

LOVE alone is capable of uniting living beings in such a way as to complete and fulfill them, for it alone takes them and joins them by what is deepest in themselves.

—Pierre Teilhard du Chardin

Traveling in the company
of those we **LOVE**
is home in motion.

—Leigh Hunt

106

107

LOVE in its essence

is spiritual fire.

—Emmanuel Swedenborg

For life, with all its
yields of joy and woe
Is just a chance o' the prize
of learning **LOVE.**

—Robert Browning

108

LOVE is a little word;

people make it big.

109

110

LOVE is the
medicine for most of
mankind's ills.

—William Menninger

111

LOVE begets **LOVE.**

This torment is my joy.

—Theodore Roethke

Life is the **LOVE** that
reaches out, building bridges
across gulfs of uncertainty
to touch hands, hearts,
and souls in the
experience of union.

—Peter Seymour

112

113

Affection should not be too sharp eyed, and **LOVE** is not made by magnifying glasses.

—Sir Thomas Browne

We are shaped
and fashioned by
what we **LOVE.**

–Johann Wolfgang von Goethe

114

LOVE makes those young
whom age doth chill,
And whom he
finds young, keeps still.

—William Cartwright

Gravity cannot be held responsible for people falling in **LOVE.**

—Albert Einstein

LOVE comforteth

like sunshine after rain.

—William Shakespeare

The truly important things
in life—**LOVE,** beauty,
and one's uniqueness—
tend to be overlooked.

—Pablo Cassals

119

LOVE doesn't make
the world go 'round.
LOVE is what makes the
ride worthwhile.

—F. P. Jones

Love is
being stupid together.

—Paul Valery

120

To **LOVE** and win
is the best thing;
to **LOVE** and lose
the next best.

—William Thackeray

121

LOVE doesn't save us from loneliness or hard times, but it does guide us through them.

LOVE cannot be

commanded.

—Latin proverb

LOVE is the child of
freedom, never that
of domination.

—Erich Fromm

124

125

LOVE is a mutual
self-giving that ends
in self-recovery.

—Bishop Fulton J. Sheen

LOVE makes all

hard hearts gentle.

—George Herbert

126

Many people when they fall in **LOVE** look for a little haven of refuge from the world, where they can be sure of being admired when they are not admirable, and praised when they are not praiseworthy.

—Bertrand Russell

127

LOVE is an
irresistible desire to be
irresistibly desired.

—Robert Frost

129

LOVE keeps the

cold out better

than a cloak.

–H. W. Longfellow

Life has taught us that
LOVE does not consist in
gazing at each other, but
looking outward together in
the same direction.

—Antoine de Saint-Exupery

130

131

If you are never in
pain because of **LOVE,**
you are never in **LOVE.**

O **LOVE**—why can't you leave me alone? Which is a rhetorical question meaning: for heaven's sake, don't.

—Thomas Merton

132

If you make mistakes,
if you act like a
human being—I will
LOVE you no matter.

—Leo Buscaglia

133

LOVE is not
really blind—the bandage
is never so tight but
that it can peep.

—Elbert Hubbard

135

What **LOVE**

creates lasts forever.

LOVE is the

greatest refreshment

in life.

—Pablo Picasso

136

137

Shall we make a new rule of life

from tonight: Always to try to be

a little kinder than is necessary?

—James Matthew Barrie

Give the kind of **LOVE**

you dream of receiving.

138

One friendship in a lifetime is much; two are many; three are hardly possible.

–Henry Adams

139

140

To fear **LOVE** is to
fear life, and those
who fear life are already
three parts dead.

—Bertrand Russell

Many lonely, unloved people assume finding the right person is what they need in order to **LOVE. LOVE** is up to you, not them.

—Bob Hoffman

Of all of men's inborn
dispositions there is none
more heroic than **LOVE.**
LOVE will fight no-**LOVE**
every inch of the way.

–Laurens van der Post

142

143

LOVE is not for levity,

but for the total

worth of man.

—Ralph Waldo Emerson

Success in marriage
is much more than finding
the right person; it is a matter
of being the right person.

—B. R. Brickner

144

The sound of a kiss
is not so loud as that
of a cannon, but its echo
lasts a great deal longer.

—Oliver Wendell Holmes

145

146

LOVE cures people—both the ones who give it and the ones who receive it.

–Karl Menninger

147

To **LOVE** for the sake of being **LOVED** is human, but to **LOVE** for the sake of **LOVING** is angelic.

—Alphonse de Lamartine

The happiest marriages
take place gradually, and
go on deepening all
through the life together.

—W. C. Gannett

148

149

The emotion of **LOVE** is not self-sustaining; it endures only when the **LOVERS LOVE** many things together, and not merely each other.

—Walter Lippman

What I cannot **LOVE,**
I overlook. Is that
real friendship?

—Anaïs Nin

150

For there is only misfortune

in not being **LOVED;**

there is misery

in not **LOVING.**

—Albert Camus

152

To **LOVE** I must have something I can put my arms around.

—Henry Ward Beecher

The door to the human heart can be opened only from the inside.

LOVE is letting go
of fear.

—Gerald G. Jampolsky

154

155

Some say we are responsible for those we **LOVE.** Others know we are responsible for those who **LOVE** us.

—Nikki Giovanni

LOVE is always

open arms.

—Leo Buscaglia

As soon as you cannot
keep anything from a woman,
you **LOVE** her.

—Paul Geraldy

157

LOVE is not measured
by how many times you
touch each other, but by
how many times you
reach each other.

Peace of mind is another
way of saying that you've learned
how to **LOVE,** that you have
come to appreciate the importance
of giving love in order to be
worthy of receiving it.

—Hubert Humphrey

The moment we indulge
our affections, the earth is
metamorphosed; there is
no winter and no night; all
tragedies, all ennuis, vanish.

—Ralph Waldo Emerson

160

161

LOVE, in fact, is the spiritual life; and without it, all other exercises of the spirit are emptied of content.

—Thomas Merton

In **LOVE** one has
need of being believed,
in friendship of being
understood.

—Abel Bonnard

162

To be capable of steady
friendship and lasting **LOVE**
are the two greatest proofs, not
only of goodness of heart, but
of strength of mind.

—William Hazlitt

163

164

True **LOVE** is like ghosts, which everybody talks about and few have seen.

—François de La Rouchefoucauld

LOVE is the strange
bewilderment that
overtakes one person on
account of another person.

—James Thurber

Blessed is the influence
of one true, **LOVING**
human soul on another.

–George Eliot

166

167

LOVE, and a cough,

cannot be hid.

–George Herbert

Happy times and bygone days
are never lost. In truth, they
grow more wonderful within
the heart that keeps them.

–Kay Andrew

168

Riches take wings,
comforts vanish, hope
withers away, but
LOVE stays with us.

—Lew Wallace

169

170

All we can do is
to make the best of
our friends, **LOVE** and
cherish what is good in
them, and keep out of
the way what is bad.

—Thomas Jefferson

171

LOVE can bring
the greatest joy to the
most unpleasant tasks.

LOVE demands that
I learn how to focus my
attention on the needs
of those I **LOVE.**

—John Powell

172

173

A friend's only

gift is himself.

—George Santayana

A happy marriage

is a long conversation

that always seems

too short.

174

What the heart has

once owned and had,

it shall never lose.

—Henry Ward Beecher

175

176

LOVE consists in desiring to give what is our own to another and feeling his delight as our own.

—Emmanuel Swedenborg

All **LOVE** is sweet

Given or returned

And its familiar voice

wearies not ever.

—Edmund Spencer

When **LOVE** and

skill work together,

expect a masterpiece.

—John Ruskin

178

179

For those who **LOVE,**

time is eternity.

–Henry Van Dyke

I wasn't kissing her, I was whispering in her mouth.

—Chico Marx

180

LOVE never asks
how much must I do,
but how much can I do.

—Frederick A. Agar

181

182

There is no hope
for joy except in
human relationships.

—Antoine de Saint-Exupery

183

LOVE must have

wings to fly away

from **LOVE,**

And to fly back again.

—Edwin Arlington Robinson

To **LOVE** deeply in one direction makes us more **LOVING** in all others.

—Madame Swetchine

184

185

LOVE is when the desire to be desired takes you so badly that you feel you could die of it.

—Henri de Toulouse-Lautrec

The greatest tragedy
of life is not that men perish,
but that they cease to **LOVE.**

—W. Somerset Maugham

186

Every house where **LOVE** abides and friendship is a guest, is surely home; and home, sweet home, for there the heart can rest.

—Henry Van Dyke

187

188

It's **LOVE** that
makes another's face
forever dear.

189

All enduring

LOVE must be based

on forgiveness.

In real **LOVE** you want the other person's good. In romantic **LOVE** you want the other person.

–Margaret Anderson

190

191

Loving means sharing

joy with people.

—Leo Buscaglia

We can only learn

to **LOVE** by giving.

–Iris Murdock

192

Blessed is the season
which engages the whole
world in a conspiracy of
LOVE!

—Hamilton Wright Mabie

193

Art is the accomplice
of **LOVE.** Take
LOVE away and there
is no longer art.

—Remy de Gourmant

195

To live without **LOVING** is not really to live.

—Moliere

Those who are the

hardest for me to **LOVE**

are probably those who

need my **LOVE** the most.

—William Cartwright

196

197

One word frees us of all the weight and pain of life: That word is **LOVE.**

—Sophocles

Earth's the right place
for **LOVE:** I don't
know where it's likely
to get better.

—Robert Frost

198

You gave me the greatest gift, the growth of **LOVE.** It started as a little seed and has grown into a flowering tree.

—Carolyn A. Kleintank

199

200

LOVE has

the patience

To endure

The fault it sees

But cannot cure.

—Edgar A. Guest

All for **LOVE,**

and nothing

for reward.

—Edmund Spenser

LOVE is, above all,

the gift of oneself.

—Jean Anouilh

202

203

We receive **LOVE**

roughly in proportion to

our capacity to **LOVE.**

—Rollo May

We find rest in those we **LOVE,** and we provide a resting place in ourselves for those who **LOVE** us.

—St. Bernard of Clairvaux

204

LOVE is not only
honoring the differences
between us, but building
on them to learn more
about ourselves.

205

206

Of all earthly music that which reaches farthest into heaven is the beating of a truly **LOVING** heart.

—Henry Ward Beecher

No matter what life brings you,
You'll have the strength to bear it,
As long as you have **LOVE** to give,
And someone who can share it

—Mary Louise Cheatham

The sweetest joy,

the wildest woe

is **LOVE.**

–Philip James Bailey

208

209

Let your **LOVE** be like

the misty rain, coming softly,

but flooding the river.

—Madagascan proverb

We are all born
for **LOVE**...It is the
principle of existence
and its only end.

—Benjamin Disraeli

210

Know my **LOVE,**
that I should like to
call you a thief, because
you have stolen my heart.

—Margaret of Nassau

212

LOVE possesses not nor

would it be possessed;

For **LOVE** is sufficient

unto **LOVE.**

—Kahlil Gibran

Marriage is that
relation between man
and woman in which the
independence is equal, the
dependence mutual, and
the obligation reciprocal.

—Louis K. Anspacher

Marriage is something
you have to give your
whole mind to.

—Henrik Ibsen

214

215

Come live in my heart
and pay no rent.

—Samuel Lover

Soul meets soul

on **LOVERS'** lips.

—Percy Bysshe Shelley

216

Accustom yourself
continually to make many
acts of **LOVE,** for they
enkindle and melt the soul.

—Theresa of Avila

The giving of **LOVE**

is an education in itself.

—Eleanor Roosevelt

219

LOVE is the art

of hearts, and

heart of arts.

—Philip James Bailey

If thou must **LOVE** me,

let it be for naught.

Except for **LOVE'S**

sake only.

—Elizabeth Barrett Browning

220

221

Now I know

what **LOVE** is.

—Virgil

When **LOVE** beckons you,
follow him, though his ways
are hard and steep.

—Kahlil Gibran

222

LOVE,

like Edg'd tools,

should never be

played with.

—Mary Davys

223

224

LOVE...

generally hurries us on

without consideration.

—Mary Hearne

The meeting of two
personalities is like the
contact of two chemical
substances: if there is
any reaction, both
are transformed.

—Carl Gustav Jung

LOVE consists in this,
that two solitudes protect
and touch and greet
each other.

–Rainer Maria Rilke

226

227

There is no more **LOVELY,**
friendly, and charming
relationship, communion, or
company than a good marriage.

–Martin Luther

LOVE is…born with the pleasure of looking at each other, it is fed with the necessity of seeing each other, it is concluded with the impossibility of separation!

—Jose Marti

228

LOVE cannot endure indifference. Like a lamp, it needs to be fed out of the oil of another's heart, or its flame burns low.

—Henry Ward Beecher

230

If I truly **LOVE** one person
I **LOVE** all persons, I **LOVE** the
world, I **LOVE** life. If I can say to
somebody else, "I **LOVE** you," I
must be able to say, "I **LOVE** in you
everybody, I **LOVE** through you the
world, I **LOVE** in you also myself."

—Erich Fromm

231

One does not fall
into **LOVE;** one
grows into **LOVE,** and
LOVE grows in him.

—Karl Menninger

LOVE turns one

person into two;

and two into one.

—Isaac Abravanel

232

233

It is difficult to lay aside

a confirmed passion.

—Catullus

The heart has its
reasons which reason
does not understand.

—Blaise Pascal

234

Whatever our souls
are made of, his and
mine are the same.

—Emily Brontë

235

In short I will part
with anything for
you but you.

—Lady Mary Wortley Montagu

237

Intense **LOVE** is often
akin to intense suffering.

—Francis Ellen Watkins Harper

We can do no great
things—only small things
with great **LOVE.**

–Mother Teresa

238

239

A successful marriage requires
falling in **LOVE** many times,
always with the same person.

—Mignon McLaughlin

LOVE stretches your heart and makes you big inside.

—Margaret Walker

240

LOVE will not always linger longest with those who hold it in too clenched a fist.

—Alice Duer Miller

241

Till it has **LOVED,** no man or woman can become itself.

—Emily Dickinson

It is better to remember

our **LOVE** as it was

in the springtime.

—Bess Streeter Aldrich

If you are not too long,

I will wait for you

all my life.

—Oscar Wilde

244

245

LOVE brings to life whatever is dead around us.

—Franz Rosenzweig

Our affections are our life.
We live by them;
they supply our warmth.

—William Ellery Channing

246

I **LOVE** you because I **LOVE** you, because it would be impossible for me not to **LOVE** you. I **LOVE** you without question, without calculation, without reason good or bad, faithfully, with all my heart and soul, and every faculty.

—Juliette Drout

247

Two persons **LOVE** in
one another the future
good which they aid
one another to unfold.

—Margaret Fuller

249

But the **LOVE** of offspring…tender and beautiful as it is, can not as a sentiment rank with conjugal **LOVE.**

—Elizabeth Cady Stanton

LOVE has a tide!

—Helen Fiske Hunt Jackson

250

251

LOVE is a great beautifier.

−Louisa May Alcott

My chief occupation,

despite appearances,

has always been **LOVE.**

—Albert Camus

252

LOVE understands **LOVE;**

it needs no talk.

—Francis Ridley Havergal

253

254

LOVE is the pass-key
to the heart.

–Madame Necker

255

There are only two things

that are absolute realities,

LOVE and knowledge,

and you can't escape them.

—Ella Wheeler Wilcox

LOVE is like the measles: we all have to go through it.

—Jerome K. Jerome

256

257

The most vital right is the right
to **LOVE** and be **LOVED.**

—Emma Goldman

If a man is worth **LOVING** at all, he is worth **LOVING** generously, even recklessly.

—Marie Dressler

258

And **LOVE** is worth

what it cost you,

nothing more.

—Marjorie Allen Seiffert

259

There is a sacred, secret
line in **LOVING** which
attraction and even
passion cannot cross.

—Anna Akmatova

261

It is only when we

LOVE a person that

we know him.

The first duty of **LOVE**

is to listen.

—Paul Tillich

262

263

O, tell her, brief is life
but **LOVE** is long.

—Alfred, Lord Tennyson

LOVE those who **LOVE** you.

—Voltaire

264

If ever two were one,
then surely we. If ever man
were **LOVED** by wife,
then thee.

—Anne Bradstreet

What's mine is yours,

and what is yours

is mine.

—William Shakespeare

When a match

has equal partners,

then I fear not.

—Aeschylus

Let there be spaces in

your togetherness.

—Kahlil Gibran

268

269

Can **LOVE** be controll'd by advice?

—John Gay

I saw and **LOVED.**

—Edward Gibbon

270

LOVE is the only gold.

—Alfred, Lord Tennyson

271

272

Marriage the happiest
bond of **LOVE** might be,
If hands were only joined
when hearts agree.

—George Granville, Baron Lansdowne

273

Beauty is in the
eye of the beholder.

—Margaret Wolfe Hungerford

We **LOVE** the things we **LOVE** for what they are.

—Robert Frost

274

275

She whom I **LOVE** is
hard to catch and conquer,
Hard, but O the glory of the
winning were she won!

–George Meredith

Ultimately the bond of all companionship, whether in marriage or in friendship, is conversation.

—Oscar Wilde

276

If you press me to say why I **LOVED** him, I can say no more than it was because he was he and I was I.

—Michel Eyquem Montaigne

277

278

LOVE is enough:
though the world
be a-waning,

And the woods have
no voice but the voice
of complaining.

—William Morris

Heart speaks to heart.

—John Henry, Cardinal Newman

280

281

When you **LOVED** me I gave you the whole sun and stars to play with. I gave you eternity in a single moment, strength of the mountains in one clasp of your arms, and the volume of all the seas in one impulse of your soul.

—George Bernard Shaw

I **LOVED** him for himself alone.

—Richard Brimsley Sheridan

282

To **LOVE** is to admire with the heart; to admire is to **LOVE** with the mind.

—Theophile Gautier

283

And yet, a single
night of universal **LOVE**
could save everything.

—Roland Giguere

285

Take away **LOVE** and

our earth is a tomb.

—Robert Browning

The great secret of successful
marriage is to treat all disasters
as incidents and none of the
incidents as disasters.

—Harold Nicholson

286

287

LOVE knoweth

no laws.

—John Lyly

Delicacy is to **LOVE**
what grace is to beauty.

—Madame de Maintenon

288

It is **LOVE,** not reason,

that is stronger than death.

—Thomas Mann

289

290

When you have
LOVED as she has
LOVED, you grow
old beautifully.

—W. Somerset Maugham

[LOVE is] the joy
of the good, the
wonder of the wise, the
amazement of the gods.

—Plato

They do not **LOVE**
that do not show
their **LOVE.**

—William Shakespeare

292

293

The heart that loves is always

young.

—Anonymous

Where love is concerned,
too much is not
even enough.

—Pierre-Augustin de Beaumarchais

294

Who can give
law to **LOVERS?**
LOVE is a greater
law to itself.

—Boethius

296

Great **LOVES** too

must be endured.

—Coco Chanel

297

Love is swift,
sincere, pious, pleasant,
generous, strong, patient, faithful,
prudent, long-suffering, manly,
and never seeking her own;
for wheresoever a man seeketh his
own, there he falleth from love.

—Thomas á Kempis

It is only by **LOVING**
a thing that you can
make it yours.

–George MacDonald

298

299

Two souls with
but a single thought,
Two hearts that
beat as one.

—Maria Lovell

LOVE is a

product of habit.

—Lucretius, De Rerum Natura

300

A mighty pain to **LOVE** it is,

and 'tis a pain to miss;

but of all the pains,

the greatest pain is to **LOVE,**

but **LOVE** in vain.

—Abraham Crowley

301

302

You don't marry
someone you can live
with—you marry the
person who you
cannot live without.

—Unknown

303

LOVE is but the discovery of ourselves in others, and the delight in the recognition.

—Alexander Smith

The richest **LOVE** is that
which submits to the
arbitration of time.

—Lawrence Durrell

304

305

There is no remedy for
LOVE but to **LOVE** more.

—Henry David Thoreau

LOVE is like playing the piano.
First you must learn to play by the
rules, then you must forget the
rules and play from your heart.

—Unknown

306

LOVE is not
LOVE that alters
when it alteration finds.

—William Shakespeare

307

308

Truly **LOVING** another means letting go of all expectations. It means full acceptance, even celebration of another's personhood.

—Karen Casey

The quarrels of **LOVERS** are the renewal of **LOVE.**

—Terence

We **LOVE**
being in **LOVE.**

—William Makepiece Thackeray

310

311

Each draws

to his best-**LOVED.**

—Virgil

I would like to have engraved inside every wedding band "Be kind to one another." This is the Golden Rule of marriage and the secret of making **LOVE** last through the years.

—Randolph Ray

312

There is no surprise more magical than the surprise of being **LOVED:** It is God's finger on man's shoulder.

—Charles Morgan

313

314

Before you **LOVE,**

Learn to run

through snow,

Leaving no footprints.

—Turkish proverb

315

True **LOVE** comes quietly, without banners or flashing lights. If you hear bells, get your ears checked.

—Erich Segal

LOVE and you shall
be **LOVED.** All **LOVE**
is mathematically just, as much
as the two sides of an
algebraic equation.

–Ralph Waldo Emerson

316

317

So often when we say
"I **LOVE** you" we say it with
a huge "I" and a small "you."

Among those whom I like,
I can find no common
denominator, but among those
whom I **LOVE,** I can; all
of them make me laugh.

–W. H. Auden

318

Treasure each other in
the recognition that we do
not know how long we shall
have each other.

—Joshua Loth Liebman

319

320

For, you see, each
day I **LOVE** you more,
Today more than
yesterday and less
than tomorrow.

—Rosemonde Gerard

321

There is only one

situation I can think of in which

men and women make an effort

to read better than they usually do.

[It is] when they are in **LOVE** and

reading a **LOVE** letter.

–Mortimer Adler

Be of **LOVE**

(a little) more careful

than of anything.

—e. e. cummings

323

But as a philosopher said, one day after mastering the winds, the waves, the tides and gravity, after all the scientific and technological achievements, we shall harness for God the energies of **LOVE,** and then, for the second time in the history of the world, man will have discovered fire.

—R. Sargent Shriver

LOVE talked about can be easily turned aside, but **LOVE** demonstrated is irresistible.

—W. Stanley Mooneyham

324

There is a land of the living
and a land of the dead and
the bridge is **LOVE,** the only
survival, the only meaning.

—Thornton Wilder

325

326

Beware of all the paradoxical in **LOVE.** It is simplicity which saves, it is simplicity which brings happiness…**LOVE** should be **LOVE.**

—Charles Baudelaire

Romance cannot
be put into quantity
production—the moment
LOVE becomes casual, it
becomes commonplace.

—Frederick Lewis Allen

To **LOVE** is to choose.

—Joseph Roux

328

329

It is the special quality of **LOVE**
not to be able to remain stationary,
to be obliged to increase under
pain of diminishing.

—Andre Gide

LOVE is friendship

set on fire.

—Jeremy Taylor

330

Nobody has ever measured,
not even poets, how much
the heart can hold.

—Zelda Fitzgerald

331

We walk among worlds
unrealized until we have
learned the secret of
LOVE.

—Hugh Black

333

We always believe
our first **LOVE** is our
last, and our last
LOVE our first.

—Gerge Whyte-Melville

Take hold lightly;
let go lightly. This is the
one of the great secrets
of felicity in **LOVE.**

—Spanish proverb

334

335

Two shall be born a whole wide world apart
And one day out of darkness they shall stand
And read life's meaning in each other's eyes.

—Anonymous

Never pretend to a
LOVE which you do not
actually feel, for **LOVE** is
not ours to command.

—Alan Watts

336

LOVE is admiring
with the heart.
And admiring is
LOVING with the mind.

—Madame de Staël

337

[LOVE is] the river of

life in this world.

—Henry Ward Beecher

339

Gold does not
satisfy **LOVE;** it must
be paid in its own coin.

—Dorothy DeLuzy

Him that I **LOVE,**

I wish to be free—

even from me.

–Anne Morrow Lindbergh

340

341

LOVE and hope

are twins.

—Maria Brooks

The mind may be exhausted,
but the language of the
heart is inexhaustible.

—Madame de Staël

342

LOVE is emotion in motion.

We can only learn to

LOVE by **LOVING.**

—Iris Murdock

343

To **LOVE** is to make
of one's heart a
swinging door.

—Howard Thurman

345

LOVERS who **LOVE**

truly do not write down

their happiness.

—Anatole France

LOVE is the only game

where two can play

and both win.

—Erma Freesman

346

347

True **LOVE** impairs nothing,

and deprives no one.

—March Cost

A successful marriage
is an edifice that must
be rebuilt every day.

—Andre Maurois

348

LOVE must be

as much a light

as a flame.

—Henry David Thoreau

349

350

The burden becomes

light that is shared

by **LOVE.**

—Ovid

351

LOVE without reverence and enthusiasm is only friendship.

—George Sand

How do I **LOVE** thee?

Let me count the ways.

I **LOVE** thee the the depth

and breadth and height

My soul can reach...

—Elizabeth Barrett Browning

352

353

Man, while he **LOVES,**

is never quite depraved.

—Charles Lamb

When we **LOVE,**

it is the heart that judges.

—Joseph Joubert

354

When you

LOVE someone,

you **LOVE** him

as he is.

—Charles Peguy

355

We like

someone because;

we **LOVE** someone

although.

—Henri de Montherlant

357

However old a conjugal union, it still garners some sweetness. Winter has some cloudless days, and under the snow a few flowers still bloom.

—Madame de Staël

LOVE is like a baby,

it needs to be

treated gently.

—Congolese proverb

358

359

LOVE is not

only letting go,

but also letting grow.

A friend **LOVES**

at all times

—Proverbs 17:17

A heart filled
with **LOVE** has
something to give.

361

362

The grand essentials in life are something to do, something to **LOVE,** and something to hope for.

—Joseph Addison

The way to **LOVE** anything is to realize that it might be lost.

–G. K. Chesterton

So much of what
we know of **LOVE** we
learn at home.

—Unknown

364

365

If you judge people,

you have no time

to **LOVE** them.

—Mother Teresa